# THE WORLD OF OCEAN ANIMALS
# SQUID

by Adeline J. Zimmerman

pogo

# Ideas for Parents and Teachers

Pogo Books let children practice reading informational text while introducing them to nonfiction features such as headings, labels, sidebars, maps, and diagrams, as well as a table of contents, glossary, and index.

Carefully leveled text with a strong photo match offers early fluent readers the support they need to succeed.

## Before Reading

- "Walk" through the book and point out the various nonfiction features. Ask the student what purpose each feature serves.
- Look at the glossary together. Read and discuss the words.

## Read the Book

- Have the child read the book independently.
- Invite him or her to list questions that arise from reading.

## After Reading

- Discuss the child's questions. Talk about how he or she might find answers to those questions.
- Prompt the child to think more. Ask: What did you know about squid before reading this book? What more would you like to learn?

Pogo Books are published by Jump!
5357 Penn Avenue South
Minneapolis, MN 55419
www.jumplibrary.com

Library of Congress Cataloging-in-Publication Data

Names: Zimmerman, Adeline J., author.
Title: Squid / by Adeline J. Zimmerman.
Description: Minneapolis: Jump!, Inc., 2022.
Series: The world of ocean animals
Includes index. | Audience: Ages 7-10
Identifiers: LCCN 2021021724 (print)
LCCN 2021021725 (ebook)
ISBN 9781636902975 (hardcover)
ISBN 9781636902982 (paperback)
ISBN 9781636902999 (ebook)
Subjects: LCSH: Squids—Juvenile literature.
Classification: LCC QL430.2 .Z56 2022 (print)
LCC QL430.2 (ebook) | DDC 594/.58—dc23
LC record available at https://lccn.loc.gov/2021021724
LC ebook record available at https://lccn.loc.gov/2021021725

Editor: Jenna Gleisner
Designer: Michelle Sonnek

Photo Credits: LUNAMARINA/iStock, cover, 3; tswinner/iStock, 1; Reinhard Dirscherl/Alamy, 4; Global_Pics/iStock, 5; NaturePicsFilms/Shutterstock, 6-7; Martin Prochazkacz/Shutterstock, 8; Thomas Marti/Getty, 9; Fred Bavendam/Minden Pictures/SuperStock, 10-11; Aleksei Permiakov/Getty, 12-13; WaterFrame/Alamy, 14; Solvin Zankl/NaturePL/SuperStock, 15; blickwinkel/Alamy, 16-17; Laura Dts/Shutterstock, 18-19; Stubblefield Photography/Shutterstock, 20-21; eye-blink/iStock, 23.

Printed in the United States of America at Corporate Graphics in North Mankato, Minnesota.

# TABLE OF CONTENTS

# CHAPTER 1

## SPEEDY SWIMMERS

What sea creature has eight arms but isn't an octopus? This ocean animal is a squid!

Squid are similar to octopuses. Both are **cephalopods** and **invertebrates**. Their bodies are soft.

siphon

mantle

A squid's body is called a **mantle**. It is long and shaped like a tube. To swim, a squid draws water into its mantle. Then it shoots a jet of water out of its **siphon**. This moves the squid through the water.

**DID YOU KNOW?**

Squid are fast swimmers. They can swim up to 25 miles (40 kilometers) per hour! They are the fastest invertebrates in the ocean.

# CHAPTER 2

## PREDATOR AND PREY

Swimming quickly helps squid escape **predators**. Large fish, sharks, and whales all hunt squid. But squid have a secret weapon.

sperm whale

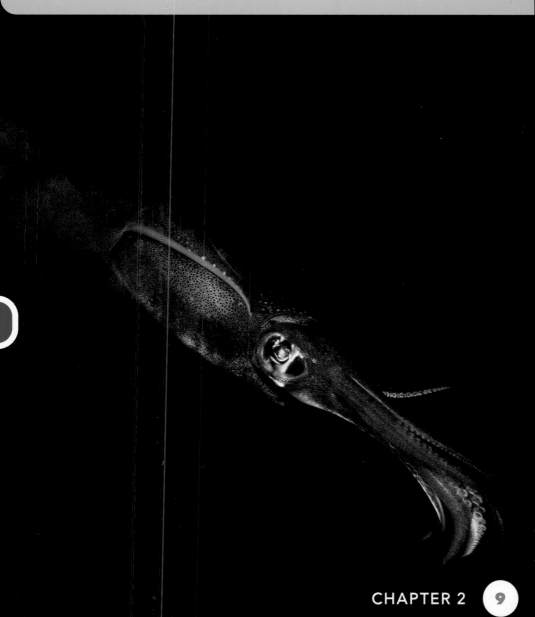

They can shoot ink! If a squid **senses** danger, it shoots ink out of its siphon. The cloud hides the squid. It confuses the predator. Then the squid can speed away and escape.

Speed also helps squid catch **prey**. Squid are **carnivores**. They hunt fish, shrimp, and other squid. Some even attach to and eat small whales! **Suction cups** on their arms help them catch and hold onto prey. Then two **tentacles** push the prey into its mouth. The mouth is in the middle of the arms. It has a sharp beak that can break shells.

# TAKE A LOOK!

What are a squid's body parts called? Take a look!

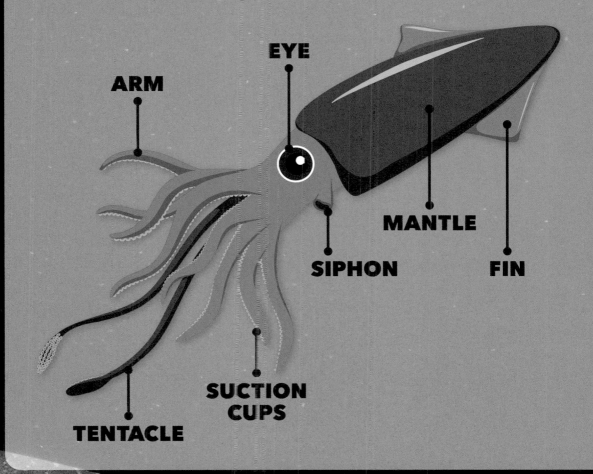

ARM

EYE

MANTLE

FIN

SIPHON

SUCTION CUPS

TENTACLE

Good eyesight also helps squid. Their large eyes help them see objects even in dark water. Scientists think they may even be able to see in color.

## DID YOU KNOW?

Giant and colossal squid are the largest kinds of squid. They can grow to be more than 40 feet (12 meters) long! Their eyeballs are the largest in the animal kingdom. They are the size of soccer balls!

eye

# CHAPTER 3

## COLORFUL CREATURES

There are more than 300 squid **species**. Many live in very deep, dark water. This makes them hard for scientists to study. There is a lot we don't know about them.

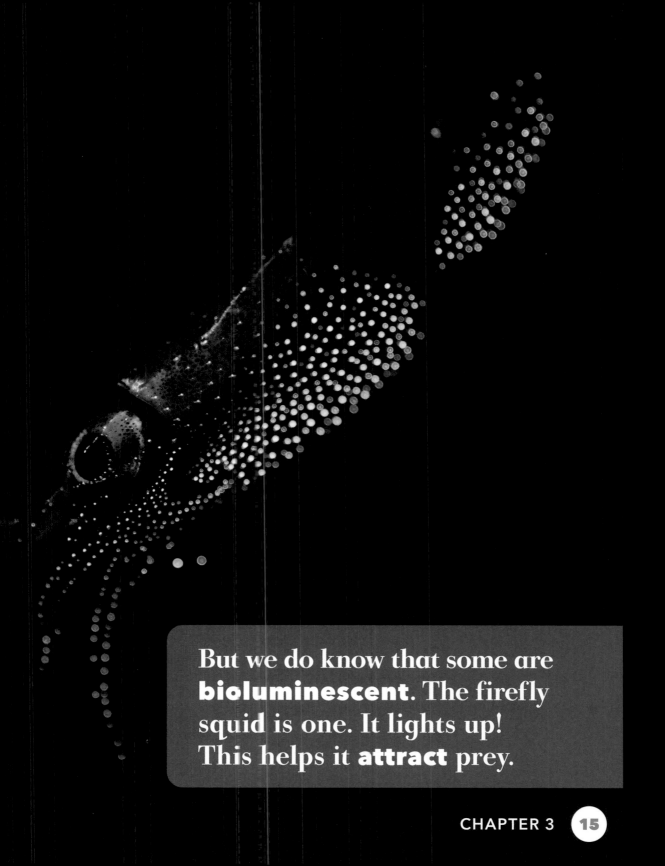

But we do know that some are **bioluminescent**. The firefly squid is one. It lights up! This helps it **attract** prey.

We know squid can change color. **Pigments** in their skin change from brown to red or many other colors! Many have spots. Some shimmer. Bright colors warn predators to stay away.

One kind of squid we know more about is the bigfin reef squid. Why? It lives near the coast in shallow water. It is easier for scientists to study.

# TAKE A LOOK!

Where do bigfin reef squid live? Take a look!

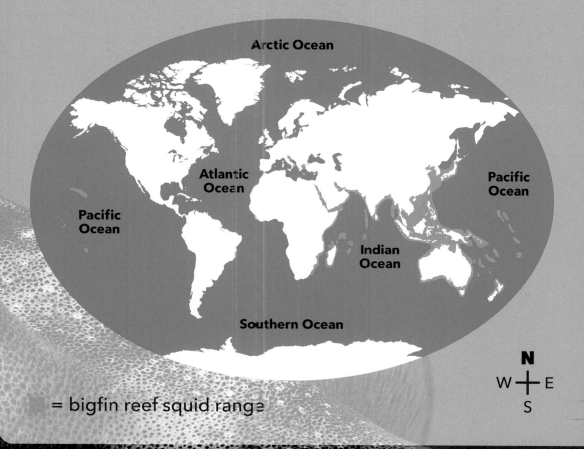

= bigfin reef squid range

Most squid live alone. But they can be found in groups to produce eggs.

We have more to learn about squid. They are masters of **disguise**. They are also speedy swimmers. So learning more is tricky. What more would you like to learn about squid?

# ACTIVITIES & TOOLS

### SQUID SIPHON

Create your own squid to see how it jets through water with this fun activity!

**What You Need:**

- scissors
- ruler
- one 0.5- to 1-liter plastic bottle
- one large balloon
- one 2L plastic bottle
- tub, sink, or large bin of cold water

❶ Have an adult help you cut the top 3 inches (7.6 centimeters) off the smaller plastic bottle. Then cut a small hole in the bottom. Remove any labels.

❷ Place an empty balloon in the smaller bottle with the neck of the balloon coming out of the cut top. This is your squid!

❸ Dip the 2L bottle into the tub of water to fill it, or fill it with water from a faucet.

❹ Place the balloon opening over the 2L top, keeping the balloon empty.

❺ Squeeze the 2L bottle to fill the balloon. Your squid mantle is now full of water! Pinch the balloon neck closed. This is your squid's siphon. Slowly pull it off the 2L bottle.

❻ While still pinching the siphon shut, place the mantle and the bottle around it into the tub of water. Then let go! How does your squid swim?

# GLOSSARY

**attract:** To gain something's interest.

**bioluminescent:** Able to produce light due to chemical reactions in the body.

**carnivores:** Animals that eat meat.

**cephalopods:** Sea creatures that have arms or tentacles attached to their heads.

**disguise:** A way of hiding something, especially by changing the way it appears.

**invertebrates:** Animals that do not have backbones.

**mantle:** The main body of a squid that is made up of muscle and skin.

**pigments:** Substances that give color to something.

**predators:** Animals that hunt other animals for food.

**prey:** Animals that are hunted by other animals for food.

**senses:** Feels or becomes aware of something.

**siphon:** The part of a squid that is attached to the mantle and shoots out water and ink.

**species:** One of the groups into which similar animals and plants are divided.

**suction cups:** Round, shallow cups that press against and stick to a surface.

**tentacles:** The flexible limbs of some ocean animals.

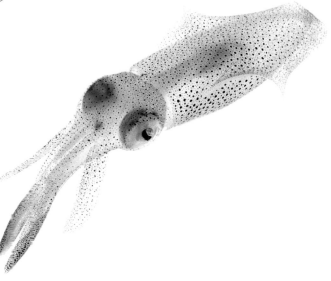

# INDEX

# TO LEARN MORE

**Finding more information is as easy as 1, 2, 3.**

**①** **Go to www.factsurfer.com**

**②** **Enter "squid" into the search box.**

**③** **Choose your book to see a list of websites.**

**FACT SURFER**